# Life in Tide Pools

## by Gus Regallo

**HOUGHTON MIFFLIN HARCOURT**
### School Publishers

PHOTOGRAPHY CREDITS: Cover © Gavriel Jecan/age fotostock. 1 Chris Pancewicz/Alamy. 2 Chris Pancewicz/Alamy. 3 © Gavriel Jecan/age fotostock. 4 Visual&Written SL/Alamy. 5 David Boag/Alamy. 6 Carolynn Shelby Method 9/Alamy. 7 © Alissa Crandall/CORBIS. 8 © Stuart Westmorland/CORBIS. 9 © Brandon D. Cole/CORBIS. 10 Jan Tove Johansson/ Getty Images.

Printed in India

ISBN-13: 978-0-547-02298-7
ISBN-10: 0-547-02298-0

2 3 4 5 6 7 8 0940 18 17 16 15 14 13 12 11 10

# Tide Pools

Millions of plants and animals live in the world's large oceans.  Plants and animals can even live in small worlds along the shore.  You can find tide pools along the beach.  If you look closely, you will find many animals!

Life can be hard for animals in a tide pool. The hot sun may dry out their water. The waves may crash in and pull animals out to sea. And birds may eat animals living in the tide pool!

# Tide Pool Plants

You can find plants in a tide pool, too. You can see clumps of seaweed. You can see brown rockweeds. They drift on the top of the water. They feel slimy. In fact, some people think they feel disgusting!

# Tide Pool Animals

Waves crash in and out of the tide pool. Each animal has a special way to survive the waves and stay in the pool. The barnacle has a simple way to survive. It makes its own glue! The glue keeps the barnacle in one place, even during a storm.

These mussels wrapped themselves to a rock with threads. Then the threads hardened onto the rock. The threads are a gooey kind of glue. It keeps them safely inside the tide pool.

A crab has fewer choices. It has to crawl under rocks to survive. The rocks hide the crab from waves and from hungry birds, too!

A starfish has feet on its arms! The rows of feet have suction cups that help the starfish move. The suction cups also help it stay in place when waves come into the pool.

The anemone looks like a flower. But don't decide to touch it! The anemone can sting just like a jellyfish. The parts that look like flower petals are stinging tentacles!

Plants and animals in a tide pool are beautiful and interesting. But don't take them out of the tide pool. Being in the water keeps them healthy and strong. If you take them out, they will get weaker and die. If you get a chance to explore a tide pool, just look closely. You will see a very special, tiny world.

# Responding

**Fact and Opinion** What facts and opinions are in *Life in Tide Pools*? Copy and complete the chart below.

| Facts | Opinions |
|---|---|
| A barnacle makes its own glue. | The anemone looks like a flower. |
| ? | ? |
| ? | ? |

## Write About It

**Text to Self** Which tide pool animal do you think is the most interesting? Write a few sentences that summarize what makes that animal interesting. Use one or two adverbs to tell how the animal does something special.

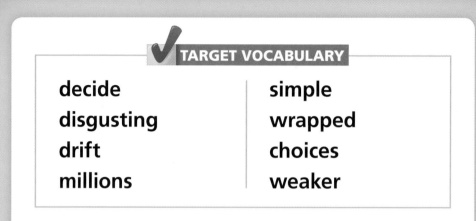

| | |
|---|---|
| decide | simple |
| disgusting | wrapped |
| drift | choices |
| millions | weaker |

**TARGET SKILL** **Fact and Opinion** Tell if an idea can be proved or is a feeling.

**TARGET STRATEGY** **Monitor/Clarify** Find ways to figure out what doesn't make sense.

**GENRE** **Informational text** gives facts about a topic.

12